THE TASSEL IS WORTH THE HASSLE

GIBBS SMITH
TO ENRICH AND INSPIRE HUMANKIND

What feels
like the end
is often the
beginning.

THIS IS the PART
WHERE YOU
FIND OUT
WHO YOU ARE.

Strive to be your best version of you.

THE TASSEL IS WORTH THE HASSLE.

Listen to your intuition.

DON'T JUST FLY—SOAR!

To uncharted waters and undreamed shores.

YOU
DID IT!

LIFE IS A CANVAS, SO GO THROW ALL THE PAINT YOU CAN AT IT.

It may be hard,
but it's never
impossible.

Go.
And set the
world on fire.

Dreams don't
work unless
you do.

ThIS IS the beginning Of anything you want.

Take a nap,
you deserve it.

Remember, knowledge is power, so never stop learning.

Change the
world?
If not you,
then who?

YOU THOUGHT GRADUATING WAS TOUGH? WAIT UNTIL YOU GET A BOSS.

MAKE YOUR MARK
ON THE WORLD!

Keep on knocking and soon doors will start opening.

Why be a copy when you can be an original?

Don't forget
to thank the
little people.

FIND YOUR PATH
AND LET THE
ADVENTURES
BEGIN.

EASY?
NO.
WORTH It?
YES.

You've got the world by a string, so hang on: it's gonna be a wild ride!

Don't ever be too proud to ask for help.

NEVER
STOP
READING!

NOBODY ELSE'S FOOTSTEPS WILL LEAD EXACTLY TO WHERE YOU ARE GOING.

Some people drink from the fountain of knowledge, others just gargle. I'm so glad you drank! ConGradulations!

NO LIMITS.
NO FEAR.

School may be
over, but your
real education
has only just
begun.

ARE YOU READY TO PARTAY!!!

Be that hERO someone can LOOK UP to.

EXPAND YOUR HORIZONS AND WIDEN YOUR CIRCLE OF FRIENDS.

Get out there and make some waves.

Time to write your own story.

The best way to predict your future is to create it.

MEET YOUR COMPETITION.

BE PREPARED FOR ANYTHING!

First Edition
22 21 20 19 18   5 4 3 2 1

1.800.835.4993 orders
www.gibbs-smith.com

Copyright © 2018 Gibbs Smith

Written by Anita Wood
Designed by Sky Hatter
Printed and bound in Hong Kong.

All rights reserved. No part of this
book may be reproduced by any means
whatsoever without written permission
from the publisher, except brief portions
quoted for purpose of review.

Gibbs Smith books are printed on either
recycled, 100% post-consumer waste,
FSC-certified papers or on paper produced
from sustainable PEFC-certified forest/
controlled wood source. Learn more at
www.pefc.org.

Published by
Gibbs Smith
P.O. Box 667
Layton, Utah 84041

Library of Congress Control Number:
2017950585
ISBN 978-1-4236-4900-7

Photo Credits

Photos from Shutterstock, as follows:

Hintau Aliaksei, 51

GUDKOV ANDREY, 70-71

apple2499, 35

bluedog studio, 43

Willyam Bradberry, 15

buddhawut, 76

Steve Collender, 12

Merrimon Crawford, 3

Paolo Cremonesi, 36

Ellerslie, 4

Ezzolo, 67

Fotontwerp, 22-23

geertweggen, 52

Gumpanat, 28

IrinaK, 63

Jag_cz, 48-49

Anan Kaewkhammul, 32-33

Keattikorn, 44-45

Iuliia Khabibullina, 56

KikoStock, 8, front cover

Irina Kozorog, 27, 72

Eduard Kyslynskyy, 16-17

LindyCro, 31

praphab louilarpprasert, 11

Alexander Mazurkevich, 68

otsphoto, 79

PHOTO FUN, 60

Photobank gallery, 74-75

Pixeljoy, 20-21

Procy, 24

Ksenia Ragozina, 7

Reddogs, 64-65

rickyd, back cover

Standa Riha, 46-47

nate samui, 38-39

surowa, 19

TalaZeitawi, 59

Miguel Urbelz, 40

wisawa222, 55